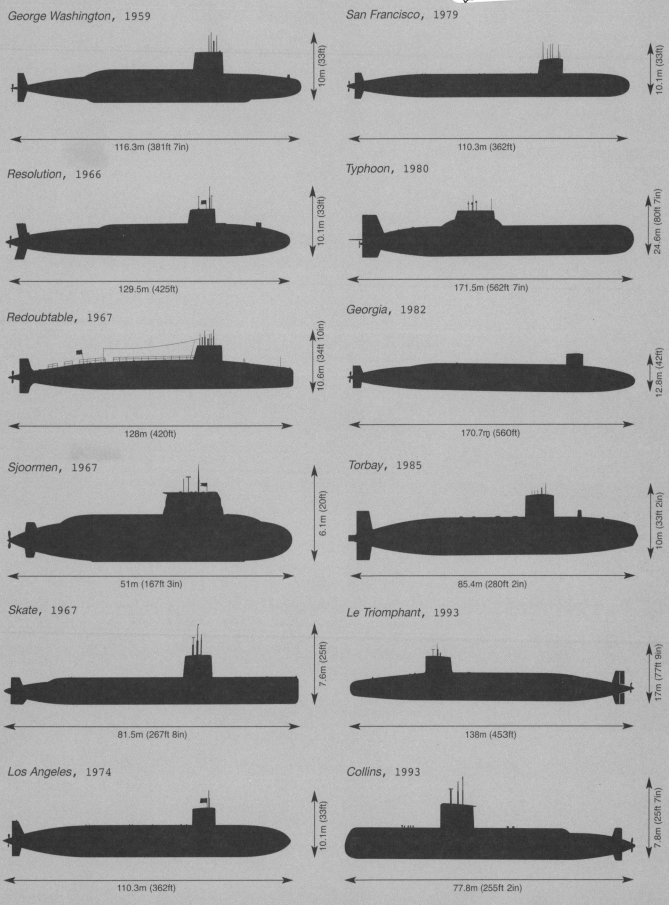

George Washington, 1959

10m (33ft)

116.3m (381ft 7in)

San Francisco, 1979

10.1m (33ft)

110.3m (362ft)

Resolution, 1966

10.1m (33ft)

129.5m (425ft)

Typhoon, 1980

24.6m (80ft 7in)

171.5m (562ft 7in)

Redoubtable, 1967

10.6m (34ft 10in)

128m (420ft)

Georgia, 1982

12.8m (42ft)

170.7m (560ft)

Sjoormen, 1967

6.1m (20ft)

51m (167ft 3in)

Torbay, 1985

10m (33ft 2in)

85.4m (280ft 2in)

Skate, 1967

7.6m (25ft)

81.5m (267ft 8in)

Le Triomphant, 1993

17m (77ft 9in)

138m (453ft)

Los Angeles, 1974

10.1m (33ft)

110.3m (362ft)

Collins, 1993

7.8m (25ft 7in)

77.8m (255ft 2in)

SUBMARINES

Explore underwater vessels from the early days to the present

PaRragon

Bath · New York · Singapore · Hong Kong · Cologne · Delhi · Melbourne

Introduction

Submarines are used in conflicts throughout the world; they are a vital part of modern-day warfare. This book will examine how they started off as an idea in the sixteenth century to how they have become essential vessels that patrol the seas.

LEFT: USS *Florida* is an Ohio-class ballistic missile submarine. The Ohio-class ship is the largest type of submarine ever constructed for the U.S. Navy.

A more effective method of depth control was necessary. As early as 1580, some inventors already understood the basic concepts of displacement and buoyancy, and these ideas were applied in various ways. Some experimental submariners tried to create a boat with a displacement that could be altered, simply by sliding sections of the hull in and out. The realization emerged that, by fitting compartments into a hull that could be flooded, it was possible to ballast the boat to the point where it would sink, or to pump air into the ballast tanks so the water was displaced. Early experimenters tried to use collapsible compartments or watertight bags, squeezing water out rather than pumping air in. This was mainly because of the limitations of the technology available at the time. The method was not effective, though it represented a move in the right direction.

Displacing water with air effectively lightened the boat and caused it to rise to the surface. By carefully controlling the amount of water and air in the tanks, it was possible to create "neutral buoyancy." In this state, the vessel would remain at its current depth. Hydroplanes, which could be angled up and down, provided additional control. Just as the vessel's rudder caused it to turn, the hydroplanes angled the boat up or down and allowed fine control of its depth. However, a boat had to be moving reasonably quickly before hydroplanes had any effect, and that, in turn, required solving the propulsion problem.

Propulsion Systems

Hand-powered submersibles proved to have rather limited capabilities whatever means of final drive were employed. There were really two options—oars or screws. Attempts to build oar-powered submarine boats were not effective despite some clever innovations, such as self-feathering oars. On a conventional boat, it was normal to lift the oars out of the water when returning to position for another stroke. This is impossible on an underwater boat, potentially resulting in the ludicrous situation where a submersible simply moved back and forth in place as the oarsmen struggled. This problem was solved by creating oars that turned themselves sideways to reduce drag on the forward stroke. Though clever, this did not solve the fundamental problems with oar power.

A screw, or propeller, was a much better option. A screw could be driven by one or more men turning handles or operating pedals, and in some cases was powered by crewmembers walking in treadmills. Screws were found to be an effective means of underwater propulsion and remained in use once engines to power them became available. Various forms of engine were tried. Steam plants never really worked in submarines, though it could be argued that a nuclear boat that uses a reactor to power a steam turbine is a steam-powered submarine, at least of a sort. Traditional furnace-powered steam plants often made the boat too hot for the crew, and attempts to use steam power on the surface and "residual steam" for underwater movement were not successful.

In the end it was the internal combustion engine, driven by gasoline or diesel, that powered most early submarines. Instead of driving the

LEFT: High-quality construction is vital to a submarine. Any weak point can cause the hull to fail, dooming the vessel.

propeller shafts directly from the engines, it was found to be more effective to use an electric motor to drive the shafts. This, in turn, was powered by batteries charged by the diesel motor. The chief advantages to this arose from the fact that the boat could run on battery power when submerged. This was not only quieter but it also used up less air.

Schnorkel Invention

This diesel-electric system meant that early submarines were much slower underwater than they were on the surface, and tended to operate as surface craft that could submerge when needed, rather than true submarines. The invention of the schnorkel, which allowed the submarine to take in air while keeping the hull submerged, was an important step forward. However, the problem of needing air for the engines was not really solved until the advent of nuclear power. A nuclear boat can remain underwater for months at a time, using recycling systems to clean the air inside for the crew to breathe.

Nuclear power is not acceptable to all nations, and in recent years new technologies have appeared that parallel the capabilities of a nuclear boat while using more conventional power. These are grouped under the heading of AIP (Air-Independent Propulsion) systems.

An attempt at an AIP system was made during World War II, using hydrogen peroxide to provide oxygen to run a diesel engine. Hydrogen peroxide is an extremely dangerous material, however, and while this system worked, it was highly prone to accidents.

A rather more useful system is to run a conventional diesel engine using a mixture of liquid oxygen and the engine's own exhaust fumes. This is known as a closed-cycle engine. It is not truly air-independent because it needs oxygen, but it is stored on board rather than being brought in from the outside environment. Liquid oxygen is stored in a "torus," comprising a tube wound vertically around the pressure hull. There are other possible variations on this theme, but most require the boat to

LEFT: The Swedish Gotland class were the first submarines in the world to employ an Air-Independent Propulsion (AIP) system.

BELOW: Buoyancy is controlled by flooding compartments in the outer hull, or by forcing water out using compressed air.

1 The vessel at full buoyancy, sitting on a cushion of air in the ballast tanks.
2 Main vents open; air rushes out, water rushes in destroying positive buoyancy.
3 The submarine sinks and achieves neutral buoyancy. Main vents are shut.
4 High-pressure air is blown into the ballast tanks and expels the water.
5 The submarine, now lighter (less dense), begins to rise.
6 The submarine is back on the surface, fully buoyant.

carry a store of liquid oxygen for use as an oxidant. The effect—to greatly extend underwater endurance—is the same in all cases.

Sensors

Some submarines have glazed windows to see out of, usually accompanied by powerful lights, but the sensor system of choice is sonar. Sonar relies on the propagation of sound waves through water to build up a picture of what is ahead of, around, and underneath the submarine.

When it was first invented, sonar was given the name ASDIC by the British. There are various suggestions as to what this acronym stood for. The most likely is that it arose as a contraction of the code names given to some components to preserve secrecy, though it was later claimed that it came from Allied Submarine Detection Investigation Committee, an organization that itself appears to be fictional. Whatever the origins of the term, it was soon replaced with the more pragmatic sonar (SOund NAvigation and Ranging). Sonar can be used in "active" or "passive" mode.

Passive sonar systems and hydrophones can be used to listen for sounds around the boat and to build up a picture of what is going on outside. Passive sonar does not, by definition, have emissions that can be picked up by another vessel. This makes it a useful way to search for hostile craft while (hopefully) remaining undetected. All vessels make at least some noise that can be detected by a passive sonar unit with enough sensitivity.

Reducing noise is an important part of submarine design because it both reduces the chances of being detected and increases the effectiveness of onboard sonar units. Under normal conditions a submarine will make a certain amount of noise, but this can be reduced by shutting down nonessential systems, moving slowly, and avoiding

RIGHT: The periscope allows personnel to observe above the surface without exposing the submarine.

accidental noise. The latter can be caused by crew activities that range from conversation to striking metal tools against the submarine's components. The term "silent running" refers to the strenuous attempts made by early submariners to eliminate noise during combat conditions.

Active sonar emits sound pulses (the distinctive "pings" forever associated with submarines) and detects their return. Sound travels well through water and is reflected by objects. Active sonar can be used for navigation, seabed mapping, and finding fish as well as searching for a target to attack. It does, however, announce the presence of the emitting vessel to any hostiles in the area.

Using sonar is anything but simple. Temperature variations and changes in pressure and salinity in the water cause sound waves to distort and sometimes even reflect them. One of the most important underwater features to a sonar operator is the thermocline, or "the layer." This is an inversion layer where water at different temperatures meets. The sudden change in water density is small but can be enough to bounce sound waves off, rather than allow them to continue in a straight line.

The thermocline can hide a vessel by bouncing sonar pulses emitted on the other side of the layer. Or, it can allow a target to be detected at great distances thanks to what is known as a

BELOW: A crewman operates sonar aboard the Ohio-class, guided-missile submarine USS *Florida* in May 2006.

convergence zone, caused by reflection of sound waves. All this complicates the interpretation of sonar data. Drawing the right conclusions can be a matter of life and death to naval submariners (see pages 70–71 for more on sonar).

Submarine Weapons

Even though the ability to travel underwater allowed submarines to approach other vessels undetected for an attack, the question of how to make that attack was a tricky one. Early submarines could not mount cannons on deck, so some other means had to be found.

One option was to use the submarine to sneak close to an enemy vessel and attach an explosive charge with a timed detonator. This was risky, but offered an inferior navy the chance to strike at a more powerful force.

Once guns that fired an all-in-one shell (and were not so prone to wetness) were invented, submarines became capable of mounting a useful gun armament. Up until the end of World War II, submarines often engaged their targets on the surface with deck guns. However, this practice was never very efficient and modern submarines use only underwater weapons. Some can lay mines, but the usual weapon is the torpedo. The term "torpedo" was first applied to the weapon we now call a mine, but with the invention of the "automotive torpedo," the term was hijacked to refer to the self-propelled weapon we know today.

Torpedoes deliver an explosive charge at a distance. Depending on the type, they may attempt a contact explosion or detonate under the target vessel. Originally torpedoes were unguided and not very reliable, but gradually a range of homing and guided torpedoes were developed that allowed an attack to be made with precision from very far off. Torpedoes are not much faster than most surface vessels, so an attack with unguided torpedoes is difficult. It is necessary to calculate where the

ABOVE: A Trident submarine-launched missile. The chief advantage of a submarine-mounted nuclear arsenal is that launch platforms are very difficult to locate.

target will be when the torpedoes arrive and aim for that point. This is termed a "firing solution." The solution can be ruined if the target ship changes course, resulting in a miss. Modern torpedoes either home in on the target, or else can be guided by signals fed down a fiber-optic cable from the launching vessel.

Some submarines can launch missiles, either from their torpedo tubes or from compartments in the hull. The weapons themselves range from short-range, antiship missiles through to cruise missiles for land attack and intercontinental ballistic missiles. There are also antiaircraft missile systems available for submarines, allowing them to attack antisubmarine helicopters instead of simply sneaking away (see pages 68–69 for more on weapons).

RIGHT: The MK37 torpedo (top) and the Stingray torpedo. The Stingray has a unique guidance system and a high single-shot kill probability.

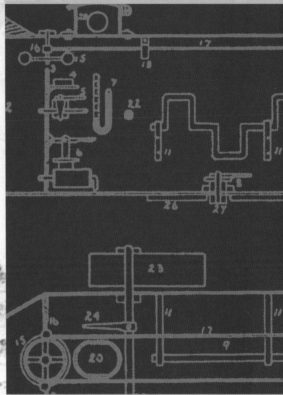

Submarines from Early Times to the Present Day

The submarine had been a dream of inventors for centuries. This book follows the development of the first experimental submarines, to the modern—potentially devastating—nuclear submarines of today.

LEFT: CSS *Hunley* was a manually propelled craft, which made the world's first successful attack using a spar torpedo. *Hunley* herself was lost in the attempt.

Early Experiments

First Attempts

In 1580, William Bourne wrote a scientific account of how a boat floated. Based on this thesis he also presented a theory of how a craft might be made to submerge and rise again under control.

Less than 50 years later, in 1623, a submersible boat was built and demonstrated by Cornelius Drebbel. Apparently Drebbel took a boat suitable to carry a crew of 12 men and enclosed it to create a watertight craft. It is not known how Drebbel dealt with the problem of buoyancy. The most likely theory is that the boat had slightly positive buoyancy and was driven down by hydroplanes of some kind while in motion. Drebbel was able to demonstrate his boat on the Thames River at a depth of about 16ft (5m).

The Rotterdam Boat

Other experiments included the 1653 Rotterdam Boat, which was an attempt to build the world's first military submersible. It was a roughly cylindrical vessel with tapered ends, making it reasonably well streamlined for underwater movement. The Rotterdam Boat did not carry any weapons but was designed to attack an enemy vessel by ramming it just below the waterline. The boat had a clever and innovative clockwork propulsion system but this was not powerful enough to move the vessel, let alone generate enough momentum for a ramming attack.

LEFT: Cornelius Drebbel built three manually powered submarines, which he successfully demonstrated on the Thames.

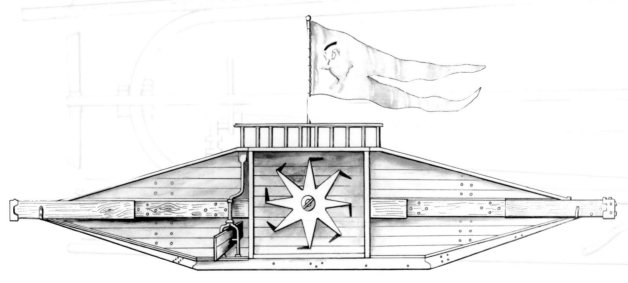

BOTTOM: The Rotterdam Boat was intended to sink enemy vessels by ramming them, but its powerplant could not generate enough power.

A Bold Concept

The less dramatic but more practical *Turtle*, invented by David Bushnell, was in many ways the typical expedient of a weak naval power facing a much stronger one. It was a bold, unconventional concept that would not have even been considered by a major naval power. *Turtle* relied on stealth and surprise to make its attack, which was to be carried out by getting underneath an anchored warship and attaching a timed charge contained in a watertight barrel towed by the craft.

Turtle was a barrel-shaped vessel propelled by two hand-cranked screws. It was designed to remain submerged a little below the surface and controlled its depth with a vertical screw. Horizontal movement was provided by the second screw, with guidance from the craft's small rudder. In 1776, *Turtle* attacked a British warship in New York harbor but was unable to attach the charge. However, the craft and its intrepid operator, Sergeant Ezra Lee, did make their escape.

Basic Principles

The early inventors understood the basic principles of the naval submarine, even if the technology to build an effective one did not at the time exist. Their boats solved the problems of buoyancy control in two ways: controllable ballast and the use of hydroplanes as a sort of rudder for vertical direction. Both of these methods are still in use today, albeit in an immensely refined form.

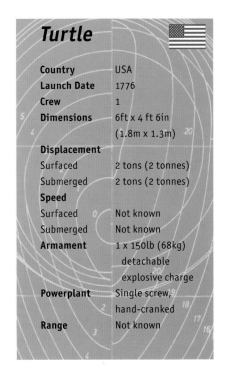

Turtle	
Country	USA
Launch Date	1776
Crew	1
Dimensions	6ft x 4 ft 6in (1.8m x 1.3m)
Displacement	
Surfaced	2 tons (2 tonnes)
Submerged	2 tons (2 tonnes)
Speed	
Surfaced	Not known
Submerged	Not known
Armament	1 x 150lb (68kg) detachable explosive charge
Powerplant	Single screw, hand-cranked
Range	Not known

BELOW: The *Turtle*, although primitive in the extreme, was the world's first workable combat submarine.

The hull was ballasted to have neutral buoyancy, floating just below the surface.

Small portholes provided the operator with a very limited view of his surroundings, making moving difficult.

Propulsion was via a hand-cranked screw, an exhausting process for the single operator.

Nineteenth-century Developments

The name *Nautilus* is popularly associated with submarines thanks to the fiction of Jules Verne, but the first *Nautilus* was built by Robert Fulton for the French navy. He offered to operate *Nautilus* as a privateer in return for a bounty paid for every enemy vessel sunk.

Nautilus was capable of about 4 knots and operated at a depth of up to 19ft (6m). It could remain submerged for up to six hours, obtaining air by means of hoses attached to a floating buoy on the surface. *Nautilus* had a sail for use on the surface and was intended to attack by attaching an explosive charge. *Nautilus* seemed promising in trials and had some interesting features, including the ability to trim the boat by pumping air into water-filled ballast tanks. However, during several attempted attacks on British vessels, the craft was easily evaded and the French navy lost interest. Fulton offered *Nautilus* to the British instead, who were equally unimpressed.

Brandtaucher

The submarine *Brandtaucher* was created to attack the Danish fleet, then blockading Kiel. It was built of iron and propelled by men walking in treadmills. On its first outing *Brandtaucher* was marginally successful—Danish warships retreated when it appeared—but on its second voyage the boat went out of control and became stuck in mud on the bottom. *Brandtaucher*'s crew escaped by waiting for pressure to equalize inside the vessel so that the hatch

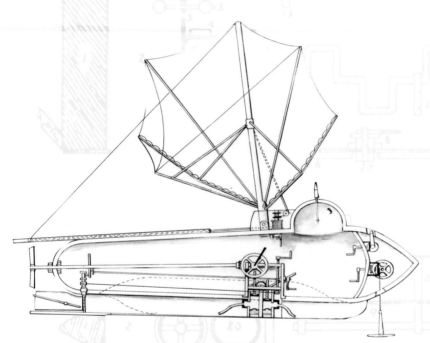

ABOVE: *Nautilus* was a step in the right direction, and demonstrated the use of several important concepts, such as water-filled ballast tanks.

BELOW: The *Intelligent Whale* demonstrated the ability to convey a diver close to the target, which was then attacked with a demolition charge.

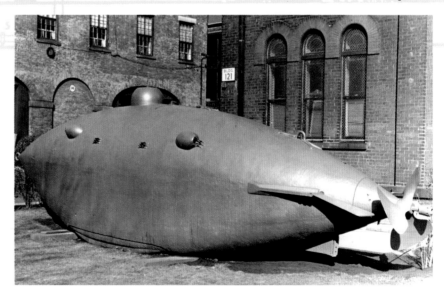

could be forced open, and swam to the surface some 30ft (10m) above.

Somewhat more successful was *Diable Marin*, which was demonstrated on more than 100 occasions. It could accommodate 16 people. On one occasion it carried a small brass band, which played the Russian national anthem in honor of the Czar's birthday. Other experiments did not go so well. In 1863, the French boat *Le Plongeur*, powered by compressed air, was tested but turned out to be uncontrollable. The U.S. equivalent, named *Intelligent Whale*, foundered on the rocks of legality. No one in the United States was prepared to authorize the project for many years and its inventor was murdered before trials were completed.

ABOVE: Fulton designed a second *Nautilus*, essentially a small conventional vessel, which could submerge.

Propulsion was by a single screw, enabling an underwater top speed of 3 knots.

A structure similar to a conning tower at the fore end of *Brandtaucher* contained the entry hatch.

Nautilus

Country	USA
Launch Date	1800
Crew	3
Dimensions	21ft x 3ft 7in (6.4m x 1.2m)
Displacement	18.7 tons (19 tonnes)
Speed	Not known
Armament	Single detachable explosive charge
Powerplant	Single screw, hand-cranked
Range	Not known

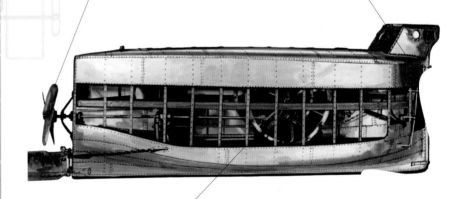

Manually powered treadmills for propulsion required a large, high boat to accommodate them.

Submarines of the American Civil War

The American Civil War was the first conflict in which submarines played a serious part. They were very much weapons of desperation and were, therefore, used by the Confederacy. The Union had little interest in novelties such as these.

The Union continued with the policy of the U.S. Navy, which had rejected a prototype submarine in 1852. Its caustic assertion was that the navy used boats that floated on water, rather than sinking under it. The Confederacy could not afford such sentiments. It was under blockade by a greatly superior naval force and needed to even the odds somehow. If submarines were useful in breaking the blockade, then they would be employed. The Confederacy, therefore, issued permission for submarines to be operated as privateers by anyone who could build one. A bounty would be paid for any Union vessel sunk.

Propelled by Hand

The first attempt was *Pioneer*, developed by Horace Hunley. A three-man, hand-propelled submarine, *Pioneer* was successfully demonstrated, managing to sink a target barge by towing a floating charge into proximity. However, *Pioneer* was scuttled when New Orleans fell to the Union. A slightly different approach created the *David*, a small vessel designed to sink the "Goliath" of a major warship. The *David* was not a submarine but attacked awash, hoping to avoid detection by being very low in the water. The usual weapon was a spar torpedo—a charge on the end of a long pole, which was rammed against the side of an enemy vessel. The *David* made several attacks but achieved little success.

CSS *Hunley*

Hunley tried again with a larger boat, which was created out of an iron boiler. Propelled by eight men cranking a hand-powered propeller and a ninth man steering, this boat had only one means of entry or egress, a small hatch

on the topside. The boat sank several times, killing Hunley himself. With remarkable persistence, the survivors kept experimenting with the boat every time it was raised, eventually renaming it CSS *Hunley*. Despite being informed that their contraption was far too hazardous for any enterprise, the crew demanded permission to try again. This time, CSS *Hunley* attacked just awash rather than submerged, using a spar torpedo. As *Hunley* approached her target, USS *Housatonic*, she was spotted by a U.S. naval ensign who subsequently gained the dubious distinction of being the first man killed by enemy action from a submarine. He was killed by the bullet of a shotgun fired from *Hunley*'s open hatch. The attack was then made and *Housatonic* was sunk, but *Hunley* herself also foundered.

CSS *David*

Country	CSA
Launch Date	1863
Crew	5
Dimensions	50ft x 6ft x 5ft (15.2m x 1.8m x 1.5m)
Displacement	Not known
Speed	Not known
Armament	1 spar torpedo
Powerplant	Steam engine
Range	Not known

Toward the Modern Submarine

In 1869, the United States Navy obtained a license to build the Whitehead Automotive Torpedo, which finally gave submarines a credible attack capability. At much the same time, the idea of powering a submarine using the internal combustion engine began to catch on.

It was still some time before a workable design for the internal combustion engine emerged. In the meantime, publication of Jules Verne's *20,000 Leagues Under the Sea* began to popularize the submarine as a vessel of war. Experimentation with powered submarines gathered pace in the late nineteenth century. Claude Goubert tried to build an electric boat, while Josiah Tuck built a steamboat powered by chemicals rather than a furnace. This vessel, named *Resurgam*, stored steam under pressure to power its underwater movement. A promising design, *Resurgam* sank while being towed on the surface.

Powered by Steam

A slightly more successful steam-powered boat, armed with a single torpedo, was built by Nordenfeldt. It was developed from the *Resurgam* design. Nordenfeldt's boat was bought by the Greek navy but proved extremely difficult to control. When the improved prototype *Nordenfeldt II* sank on trials and *Nordenfeldt III* ran aground en route to delivery, the concept quietly faded from the scene. Meanwhile, Gustave Zede's boat *Gymnote* demonstrated that electric power was workable. However, *Gymnote* could not recharge its batteries, so it remained only a technology demonstrator. Nevertheless, Zede earned himself a place in the annals of submarine design and later boats were named in his honor. One solution to the problem of charging batteries

Gustave Zede

Country	France
Launch Date	June 1893
Crew	19
Dimensions	159ft x 10ft 6in x 10ft 6in (48.5m x 3.2m x 3.2m)
Displacement	
Surfaced	261 tons (265 tonnes)
Submerged	270 tons (274 tonnes)
Speed	
Surfaced	20 knots
Submerged	28 knots
Armament	1 x 17.7in (450mm) torpedo tube
Powerplant	Single screw electric motor
Range	Not known

RIGHT: Named after her inventor, *Gustave Zede* was probably the first submarine to mount an effective periscope.

was demonstrated by George Baker's experimental vessel, which used a steam engine to drive a dynamo and thus keep the batteries replenished. Other novel designs included *Argonaut*, which had wheels to allow it to drive on the bottom when necessary.

Modern Boats

At the very end of the century, modern boats began to emerge. The French boat *Gustave Zede* was able to conduct a successful torpedo attack on exercise, which prompted interest in a true military submarine. It also managed more than

2,500 dives without meeting with disaster. *Gustave Zede* was important in other ways too—she had a conning tower on top where lookouts could stand when she surfaced, and a central control room just beneath it. *Gustave Zede* was followed by *Narval*, which used a diesel engine.

ABOVE: *Argonaut* survived in the open sea in a storm that sank many other vessels. The designer was congratulated in a letter from Jules Verne.

ABOVE RIGHT: *Gymnote* made more than 2,000 dives under electric power, proving the concept for later, more developed vessels. She eventually sank at Toulon in 1907.

Holland's Boats

The name of John Holland is prominently associated with submarines. Holland started out with a proposal to the U.S. Navy for a boat, which was rejected. His ideas were taken up by the Fenians—Irish rebels who were willing to support Holland's experiments.

Holland 1

The first Holland boat was named *Holland 1* and worked well enough that a larger vessel was constructed for combat purposes. This was *Fenian Ram* and seemed promising. However, the project collapsed in internal bickering. Undeterred, Holland formed his own company and built a submarine named the *Zalinski Boat*. It was damaged at launch and the project collapsed along with the company. Next, Holland entered a U.S. navy design competition and won it, only to have the project derailed twice by political decisions. Finally, he obtained funding to build *Plunger*, a torpedo-armed boat that the Navy insisted must be powered by steam. This made the boat too hot for the crew. Holland had argued strenuously against steam power but was overruled by naval officers who had no experience with submarines and (according to Holland) lacked any understanding of how to build one.

Plunger was followed by the gasoline-engined *Holland VI*, which mounted a compressed-air-powered dynamite gun as well as a single torpedo. The *Holland VI* design was bought by the U.S. Navy, and other navies began placing orders for small numbers. Among those impressed by the boats' performance was Admiral Sir John "Jacky" Fisher, who for a time advocated a navy made up entirely of submarines and torpedo boats. However, the U.S. Navy remained dubious. Some officers saw the boats as mere novelties, while others speculated that had the enemy possessed submarines in the recent U.S.–Spanish war, they might have prevented the capture of Manila.

Legal Challenges

Holland had formed several companies to build submarines, but just as he finally achieved success with the Electric Boat Company, he was edged out by internal politics. Holland made one final attempt and sold some improved designs but was put out of business by legal challenges from Electric Boat.

RIGHT: John Philip Holland spent most of his working life developing submarines. Much of his research was funded by the Fenian Brotherhood, who hoped to create a weapon to be used against Britain.

Holland VI	🇺🇸
Country	USA
Launch Date	May 1897
Crew	7
Dimensions	53ft 3in x 10ft 3in x 11ft 6in (16.3m x 3.1m x 3.5m)
Displacement	
Surfaced	63 tons (64 tonnes)
Submerged	75 tons (76 tonnes)
Speed	
Surfaced	8 knots
Submerged	5 knots
Armament	1 x 18in (457mm) torpedo tube; 1 x pneumatic gun
Powerplant	Single screw, gasoline engine/electric motor
Range	Submerged: 40nm (74km) at 3 knots

The *Holland VI* had a streamlined hull form that allowed a top speed of 5 knots underwater, or 8 knots on the surface.

Armament included one 18-in (457-mm) torpedo tube and a pneumatic gun.

Operating the boat and its weapons required a crew of seven.

RIGHT: *Holland 1* was the first submarine commissioned by the British Royal Navy; she was the first of six boats in the *Holland* class.

German Submarines of Early World War I

It was not until 1906 that Germany obtained its first Unterzeeboot, or U-Boat. *U-1* was a credible weapon of war, capable of 8.7 knots underwater and 10.8 knots on the surface using kerosene engines. Armament was modest (a single torpedo tube), but *U-1* could cruise about 1,536nm (2,845km) on the surface. Germany started late with submarines but benefited from the experience of others. From the first, all German boats had twin screws powered by kerosene engines rather than the more dangerous gasoline systems favored elsewhere. Double hulls—an inner pressure hull and an outer hull carrying components that did not need to be protected from pressure—were used on all vessels.

By the outbreak of World War I, U-boats were an effective weapon. Typical armament included four 20in (508mm) torpedo tubes and a 3.4in (86mm) deck gun. Development continued at a steady pace. *U-21*, built in 1913, was about two-and-a-half times the size of *U-1* and had a cruising range of 5,500nm (10,186km). In 1915, *UB-14* scored a notable first—the sinking of another submarine. This was the British *E20*, which was ambushed in the Sea of Marmara. *E20* was on the surface at the time she was attacked. Documents captured aboard a French submarine indicated the rendezvous area used by British and French boats, allowing an attack to be set up.

Rules of Engagement

U-boats sank a number of major naval vessels, including the destruction of an entire cruiser squadron in the North Sea by *U-9*. The fear of submarine attack heavily influenced British naval thinking at sea and even prompted the fleet to move from Scapa Flow to safer bases on the west side of Scotland.

Deutschland	
Country	Germany
Launch Date	1916
Crew	56
Dimensions	213ft 3in x 29ft 2in x 17ft 5in (65m x 8.9m x 5.3m)
Displacement	
Surfaced	1,512 tons (1,536 tonnes)
Submerged	1,875 tons (1,905 tonnes)
Speed	
Surfaced	12.4 knots
Submerged	5.2 knots
Armament	None
Powerplant	Twin screw diesel engines, electric motors
Range	11,280nm (20,909km)

Deutschland could make 12.4 knots on the surface, comparable with many conventional merchant vessels.

As a warship, *U-155* carried 18 torpedoes launched from two bow tubes. She was not armed while serving as a merchant vessel.

Deutschland was essentially a blockade runner capable of submerging to sneak past patrols.

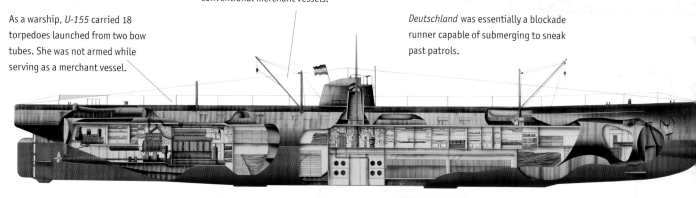

U-boats also carried out commerce raiding against merchant traffic. At first, efforts were made to comply with international law, but excessive U-boat losses prompted a number of changes in the rules of engagement (and some guidance to U-boat skippers on creative log entries) to allow boats to operate at reduced risk by using surprise attacks. It became apparent that the only viable strategy was to use unrestricted submarine warfare, sinking merchant ships without warning. By this time, the Allied blockade of Germany was causing severe shortages, and it was felt to be morally acceptable to do the same to Britain by any means necessary.

Submarine Innovations

At the beginning of the war, no means existed to track or attack a submerged submarine, but necessity forced the rapid development of technology. Surface ships were outfitted with depth charges and forward-firing mortars launching contact-fused projectiles. Attacks were guided by ASDIC—the rather primitive forerunner of today's sonar system. Even though these innovations gave the antisubmarine forces the ability to strike back, German submarines continued to take a toll of merchant traffic.

RIGHT: Few torpedoes could be carried on a submarine, so most attacks were made on the surface using deck guns.

Allied Submarines of Early World War I

Some Allied nations entered the war with large submarine fleets. Most vessels were very basic, such as the British A and B classes, and were of limited effectiveness. The D class was the first British submarine intended to undertake more than local coastal operations, and the E class had an operational range of 3,579nm (6,628km).

D-class boats helped protect troop convoys to the Continent and made offensive patrols into the Heligoland Bight. These boats were easier to operate and less prone to problems than their predecessors. Equally importantly, they could send wireless transmissions. This made them useful reconnaissance assets and permitted cooperation with surface vessels.

As the war went on, armament gradually increased with boats gaining more torpedo tubes. It became standard practice to mount rearward-facing torpedo tubes, giving the commander extra options. Underwater reloading of torpedo tubes was a relatively new technique and took considerable time, so most boats could only launch as many torpedoes as they had tubes in any one attack. Despite earlier commanders labeling the submarine as "unfair" and "un-English," British boats were aggressively handled and enjoyed considerable success against enemy shipping, including capital vessels, such as the Turkish battleship *Hairredin Barbarossa*.

European Efforts

France started the war with 62 submarines, many of which were active in the Mediterranean and the Adriatic. In April 1916, a Frimaire-class boat snuck into an Austrian harbor to torpedo a destroyer. Italian boats also took on the Austro-Hungarian navy in the Adriatic. They were small and had a short range and tended to operate on the defensive as a result.

Russian Submarines

Russia started the war with nearly 50 boats. Many were of very early designs, such as Holland- and Lake-class boats, with minimal armament. Russian submarines were active in the Baltic Sea before the Russian Revolution took the country out of the war. Italy's submarine force was mainly confined to Adriatic operations, attempting to keep the Austro-Hungarian fleet bottled up. The shallow waters of the Adriatic were difficult territory for submarines, and it was soon discovered that a submarine could be spotted from the air. However, at the time there was no air-dropped weapon available with which to attack a submerged boat.

TOP LEFT: Britain's larger D- and E-class vessels were aggressively handled and achieved notable successes during the war.

ABOVE: *Ventose*, a boat of the French Pluviose class. These vessels were powered by steam.

TOP: Torpedoes aboard a British E-class boat. Some 55 E-class boats were constructed, of which six could carry mines instead of part of their torpedo armament.

E Class

Country	United Kingdom
Launch Date	1913
Crew	30
Dimensions	181ft x 22ft 8in x 12ft 6in (55.17m x 6.91m x 3.81m)
Displacement	
Surfaced	667 tons (677 tonnes)
Submerged	807 tons (820 tonnes)
Speed	
Surfaced	14 knots
Submerged	9 knots
Armament	5 x 18in (457mm) torpedo tubes; 1 x 12-pounder gun
Powerplant	Two twin-shaft diesel engines, two electric motors
Range	3579nm (6,628km)

Allied Submarines of Late World War I

Allied submarines also improved during the course of the war, becoming faster and more capable. The British J class was designed as a counter to fast German submarines, and could make 17 knots on the surface.

The J class had six torpedo tubes and a 2.95in (75mm) gun. Few were built, but their capabilities were demonstrated when *J1* torpedoed two German battleships. In addition to surface vessel kills, British submarines sank 17 German boats, and achieved the distinction of making the first sub-on-sub kill while both vessels were submerged. This required inventing a technique for calculating a three-dimensional, torpedo-firing solution in the middle of combat.

Hunter-killers

A specialized sub-hunting submarine was developed. This was the R class. Small and fast, equipped with special sensors and armed only with torpedoes, these craft were not available early enough to make a difference, but they showed the way for the future. They can be considered the first Hunter-Killer submarines.

U.S. Designs

The USA entered World War I with 30 submarines in service. By the end of the war there were 120. U.S. boats did not contribute greatly to the war effort, though the submarine service gained considerable experience that proved useful in World War II. Some of the U.S. designs were fairly poor. Most still used gasoline engines, which were a constant explosion hazard. Others were either obsolete by the time they entered service, such as USS *Seal*, or difficult to operate. The latter included a number of boats designed by the Italian, Laurenti, which also posed problems for the builders. Conversely, some U.S. designs were both innovative and useful. Among them was the L class, which had a retractable deck gun. This reduced underwater drag and permitted a slightly higher submerged speed than otherwise. The same class demonstrated the need for U.S. boats to be able to dive faster—the L class took nearly two-and-a-half minutes to submerge. U.S. designers had not greatly worried about diving speed up to this point. The theory was that the masts of a warship could be seen far enough away to allow a leisurely dive. The advent of aircraft, coupled with operational experience under wartime conditions, changed this view and subsequent classes paid more attention to diving speed.

RIGHT: Sailors drill with the 12-pounder gun aboard a British E class boat.

ABOVE: Two R class and one H class boats. The R class was the world's first "Hunter-Killer" submarine, designed to locate and sink U-boats.

BELOW: *L-10*, a late-war British boat, sank a German destroyer in October 1918 but was then sunk by other surface vessels.

USS *L-10* 🇺🇸	
Country	USA
Launch Date	March 1916
Crew	28 officers and men
Dimensions	167ft 5in x 17ft 5in x 13ft 7in (51.03m x 5.31m x 4.14m)
Displacement	
Surfaced	450 tons (457 tonnes)
Submerged	548 tons (557 tonnes)
Speed	
Surfaced	14 knots
Submerged	10.5 knots
Armament	1 x 3in (76mm) gun; 4 x 18in (457mm) torpedo tubes
Powerplant	Twin screws, diesel/ electric motors
Range	4,500nm (8,334km)

Mediterranean. Many were of modern and capable designs. The Brin class mounted four 21in (533mm) torpedo tubes fore and the same aft, with 6 reload torpedoes, plus a 4.7in (120mm) deck gun. The Imperial Japanese Navy viewed its submarines as an adjunct to the battle fleet, operating them in squadrons as reconnaissance assets rather than as raiders. This neglect of the commerce raider role carried over into defensive thinking—the Japanese suffered heavily from submarine attacks on their merchant marine and fleet train assets.

U-47

Country	Germany
Launch Date	1938
Crew	44
Dimensions	218ft x 20ft 3in x 15ft 6in (66.5m x 6.2m x 4.7m)
Displacement	
Surfaced	753 tons (765 tonnes)
Submerged	857 tons (871 tonnes)
Speed	
Surfaced	17.2 knots
Submerged	8 knots
Armament	5 x 21in (533mm) torpedo tubes; 1 x 3.5in (88mm) gun; 1 x .79in (20mm) AA gun
Powerplant	Two-shaft diesel/ electric motors
Range	5,642nm (10,454km)

U-47 was a Type VIIC U-boat, the mainstay of the German submarine war.

The VIIC class mounted a deck gun for surface attacks, along with 14 torpedoes fired from four bow and one stern torpedo tubes.

ABOVE: *U-47* carried out 10 war patrols, sinking 32 vessels over the period of 238 days at sea. She was finally sunk, probably by two Royal Navy corvettes, in March 1941.

The hull of the *U-47* was tough enough to withstand depth-charging for extended periods.

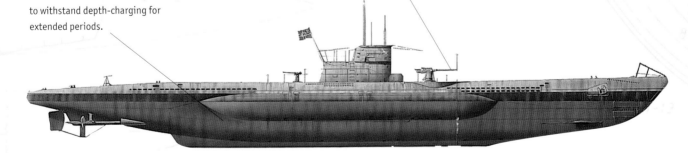

Allied Submarines of Early World War II

Many British boats of the early war were roughly equivalent in size to the Type VII U-boats. The S class, dating from the early 1930s, displaced 650 tons (590 tonnes) on the surface and carried six 21in (533mm) torpedo tubes.

The boats intended for fleet operations (in conjunction with the surface fleet) needed to be faster on the surface and tended to be larger. The 21-knot Thames class displaced 1,805 tons (1,834 tonnes) but did not carry significantly heavier armament than the S class. The French submarine fleet did not have much opportunity to contribute to the war, though Free French forces did operate a number of boats after the surrender of their government.

U.S. Developments

The U.S. Navy did not pursue submarine construction or development very vigorously in the years between wars, but greatly increased production at the start of the 1940s. The Gato class, with six bow and four stern torpedo tubes, was the standard U.S. fleet submarine at the outset of the war. The *Gatos* and subsequent classes derived from them were large—about twice the size of an Atlantic-capable U-boat.

U.S. submarines needed to operate over very long distances in the Pacific theater. They were hampered early in the war by an extremely cautious doctrine and defective torpedoes. Far more torpedoes malfunctioned than exploded even when a hit was made, and ammunition stocks were low. Submarine captains were urged to conserve ammunition rather than taking any opportunity for an attack.

This policy gradually changed, and at the same time more and better torpedoes became available. Increased aggression and weapons that actually worked resulted in an extremely effective campaign against Japanese shipping as the war continued. The USA did not enter the war until 1941, and the submarine campaign did not get going for some time afterward. Nevertheless, by the end of the war the U.S. submarine service had succeeded in crippling the Japanese merchant fleet. This cut the home islands off from vital raw materials and greatly reduced Japanese war-fighting capability in the long term.

ABOVE: The S class was designed to meet a British Royal Navy requirement for smaller boats, which were well suited to the North Sea and Mediterranean.

BELOW: The U.S. Gato class was built in large numbers and served as the basis for the later Balao and Tench classes.

USS *Gato*

Country	USA
Launch Date	1941
Crew	
Dimensions	311ft 9in x 27ft 3in x 17ft (95.02m x 8.31m x 5.18m)
Displacement	
Surfaced	1,525 tons (1,549 tonnes)
Submerged	2,386 tons (8,334 tonnes)
Speed	
Surfaced	21 knots
Submerged	9 knots
Armament	10 × 21in (533 mm) torpedo tubes, 24 torpedoes, 1 × 4in (102mm)/50 caliber deck gun; four MGs
Powerplant	4 × GM Model 16-248 V16 diesel engines, 4 × high-speed GE electric motors
Range	11,000 nm (20,372km)

Axis Submarines Of Late World War II

Most nations suffered

problems with their torpedoes early in the war. Some defects were avoidable, such as depth settings based on practice warheads that did not weigh the same as live weapons, so ran deeper than expected. This could cause a torpedo to pass beneath a vessel on the surface without detonating.

Wolf Packs

Other problems with torpedoes were technical—many simply failed to explode because their detonators were defective. Better torpedoes were accompanied by advances in submarine design and construction, as well as successful wolf-pack tactics. This idea was implemented as early as 1940 and was used throughout the war. By cooperating, a team of U-boats could ensure that at least one boat was in position to make an attack. Shifting patrol areas also paid dividends. For example, a handful of boats operating off Florida in 1942 caused severe losses to U.S. shipping, which was silhouetted against the lights of the shore.

The grim Battle of the Atlantic began in earnest in 1942, but already the tide was turning. Aircraft, using rockets, bombs, and depth charges, took an increasing toll among U-boats, especially as they transited the Bay of Biscay en route to, and from, their bases. To counter this, some boats gained increased antiaircraft armament. Their captains had a choice between crash diving and staying on the surface to fight it out. Another way of reducing submarine losses was to avoid surfacing, using a "snorkel" to obtain air for the crew and engines while the boat remained submerged. This was imperfect but it did help the U-boats maintain their primary advantage of stealth.

Hitler's New Design

In an attempt to tip the balance back in favor of his U-boats, Hitler decided to proceed with the construction of hydrogen peroxide-powered boats. These had been demonstrated some

LEFT: Hydrography developed hand-in-hand with submarine design. Accurate plotting of water conditions was of immense benefit to German U-boat commanders.

time previously but at that point it seemed that conventional boats were entirely sufficient. The new boat, designated Type XVIII, was obviously not going to be ready in time to make a difference, so a more conventional diesel-electric U-boat was based on the design. This became the Type XXI. It used the large space intended for hydrogen peroxide storage to house extra batteries, giving increased underwater range and performance. After the war, the British experimented with hydrogen peroxide-powered boats derived from wartime German experiments. They proved to be extremely hazardous to operate.

ABOVE: The Type XXI U-boat had a greatly increased battery capacity, enabling it to travel submerged for two to three days at a time.

LEFT: The schnorkel concept was in common use from 1944 onward, enabling boats to run their diesel engines while remaining submerged.

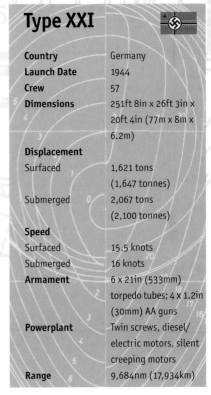

Type XXI

Country	Germany
Launch Date	1944
Crew	57
Dimensions	251ft 8in x 26ft 3in x 20ft 4in (77m x 8m x 6.2m)
Displacement	
Surfaced	1,621 tons (1,647 tonnes)
Submerged	2,067 tons (2,100 tonnes)
Speed	
Surfaced	15.5 knots
Submerged	16 knots
Armament	6 x 21in (533mm) torpedo tubes; 4 x 1.2in (30mm) AA guns
Powerplant	Twin screws, diesel/electric motors, silent creeping motors
Range	9,684nm (17,934km)

The Type XXI U-boat had a double hull. The outer hull was light and streamlined and the inner hull was made of high-carbon steel.

In addition to her main engines, the Type XXI could run silently at 3.5 knots underwater using "creeper" engines.

The Type XXI's submerged speed was actually greater than when surfaced.

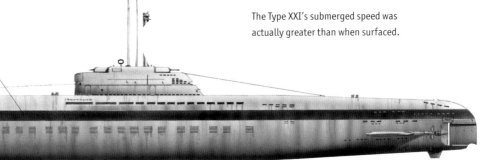

Western Attack Submarines of the Early Cold War

In the immediate postwar period, wartime designs soldiered on for a while, but gradually modern attack submarines emerged. The role of an attack submarine is to sink enemy surface ships and submarines, ideally by surprise attack. Advances were made in weaponry and sensors, while boats were made as quiet as possible.

Nuclear Power

Most nations continued to use diesel-electric boats, albeit of increasingly advanced design. Those nations that chose to pursue nuclear-powered submarines took a gamble. The development process was expensive and filled with difficulties. Once nuclear boats were available, however, their sustained high speeds and immense endurance allowed operations anywhere in the world. Nuclear boats are to some extent a return to steam power. The reactor is used to heat water to make steam, which drives a turbine that in turn generates electricity to power the boat and run the motors. There is a bank of batteries for emergency use. In many cases, submarines returned to their early role of coastal defense. One example is the Italian Enrico Toti class, a small boat designed for the shallow waters of the Mediterranean Sea. These boats were designed to lurk at choke points, where geography forced ships through a narrow channel, conducting an ambush, then sneaking away to find a new target.

Built to Endure

Some nations implemented a mix of diesel boats for shorter range operations and nuclear attack submarines for long patrols worldwide. Nuclear boats are actually more noisy than diesel submarines because they have to keep the reactor pumps running, where a diesel-electric boat powered by batteries is all but silent. However, the endurance advantage of nuclear boats offsets this factor in the eyes of many navies. In the West, greater emphasis began to be placed on hunting and sinking enemy submarines rather than surface vessels. This largely came about as a result of the threat posed by the vastly expanded Soviet submarine fleet, which seriously threatened Western merchant shipping in the event of a war.

BELOW: USS *Skate* set a number of impressive "firsts," including first transit under the North Pole and the first entirely submerged crossing of the Atlantic.

A small hull minimizes sonar cross section and makes the boat difficult to detect.

Lack of deck guns improves underwater performance and quietness.

Four 21in (533mm) torpedo tubes can launch guided torpedoes against surface or underwater targets.

ABOVE: The Italian Enrico Toti-class submarine, entering service in 1967, was designed as a small coastal vessel optimized for the shallow, cluttered waters off Italy.

USS *Skate*

Country	USA
Launch Date	1955
Crew	8 officers and 76 men
Dimensions	267ft 7in x 25ft
	(7.6m x 81.56m)
Displacement	
Surfaced	2,550 tons
	(2,590 tonnes)
Submerged	2,848 tons
	(2,894 tonnes)
Speed	
Surfaced	15.5 knots
Armament	8 × 21in (533mm)
	torpedo tubes
	(6 forward, 2 aft)
Powerplant	1 x S3W nuclear
	reactor
Range	Unlimited

Early Missile Boats to Modern Boomers

In 1942, a German U-boat successfully launched a salvo of artillery rockets from 49ft (15m) below the surface, prompting interest in missile-launching submarines. A plan to use a nuclear-tipped V2 rocket launched by a submarine against New York was drawn up, but this project was overtaken by events and never completed.

After the war, NATO and the Warsaw Pact developed the idea further. Early attempts were clumsy and only marginally effective—USS *Grayback* was capable of launching two Regulus missiles with a range of 434nm (804km). This required approaching close to a hostile coast and launching from the surface, virtually ensuring that the submarine would not escape retribution. Improvements followed quickly, with the introduction of vessels capable of carrying several missiles and launching while underwater. It has become standard practice for ballistic missiles to be carried upright in launch tubes mounted vertically in the submarine either forward or aft of the sail.

Long-Range Attack

As missile range and accuracy increased, it became possible to attack an enemy's cities from halfway around the world. This meant that missile boats no longer needed to approach an enemy coast to launch their weapons. They could hide anywhere in the oceans and strike by surprise. The main advantage of submarine-launched missiles is that they are hard to eliminate with a first strike, and so make an excellent deterrent (retaliation is certain). However, the subs must be protected from attack. Most Western powers do this by hiding them in nondescript areas of ocean; most of the crew do not know where their patrol area is, so security is easy to maintain.

Precision Strikes

The Warsaw Pact developed a strategy of creating "bastions"—sea areas bounded

USS *Grayback*

Country	USA
Launch Date	1957
Crew	87
Dimensions	273ft x 27ft 2in x 19ft (83m x 8.28m x 5.8m)
Displacement	2,768 tons (2,812 tonnes)
Speed	14 knots
Armament	8 × torpedo tubes, 1 × Regulus missile launcher
Powerplant	Not known
Range	Not known

by land on some sides and heavily
defended by attack submarines, aircraft,
minefields, and surface vessels. Some
boats are capable of launching cruise
missiles rather than strategic ballistic
weapons. Some of these weapons,
such as the Tomahawk missile, can
carry a nuclear warhead but can also
be used in a more conventional role for
precision strikes on important targets.
Therefore, the missile submarine has now
become capable of land attack, a role
traditionally performed by surface craft
armed with large guns.

ABOVE: U.S. *Halibut* was the first submarine
designed to launch missiles. Her later career
was spent as a special operations submarine
involved in espionage missions.

RIGHT: The first submarine-launched missiles
were codenamed Regulus.

BELOW: USS *Grayback* was intended to be an
attack submarine but was converted to launch
Regulus missiles.

Advanced Soviet Attack Submarines

In order to attack Western carrier battle groups more effectively and to counter increasingly advanced antisubmarine warfare (ASW) capabilities, the Warsaw Pact developed ever more potent attack submarines.

In the 1970s, the Alfa class appeared. This was a large and extremely fast nuclear attack boat, capable of 42 knots underwater and armed with a mix of nuclear and conventional torpedoes. At the time, it was thought that the Alfa could dive deep enough to evade all available torpedoes, prompting research into deep-running torpedoes that proved unnecessary. Like many such threats, it turned out that the Alfa was not so potent as it seemed—the reactors were very unreliable and maximum depth was nowhere near as deep as had been feared at first.

Reliable Diesel

Not all advanced attack boats were nuclear-powered, however. The Kilo class, which appeared in the 1980s, is diesel-powered yet capable of 24 knots underwater. These boats have met with considerable export success, granting modern attack-boat capabilities to navies that could not afford to develop their own vessels.

Before the Soviet Union broke up, very advanced boats were beginning to appear. These included the Sierra class, which has been reported as successfully

The hull was not designed for deep diving as was assumed in the West, but is capable of reaching a test depth of 1,148ft (350m).

The Alfa class had a liquid-metal reactor capable of driving the boat at 42 knots underwater.

The Alfa class featured six torpedo tubes capable of launching conventional or nuclear torpedoes.

ABOVE LEFT: The Akula-class attack submarine can use torpedoes against ships or submarines, and missiles to attack surface targets and coastal installations.

ABOVE: The Sierra class was designed for high underwater speed and stealth, with a large gap between the pressure hull and outer casing to reduce noise.

BOTTOM LEFT: The Alfa class caused grave consternation in the West because of its assumed deep-diving capabilities.

Alfa Class

Country	USSR
Launch Date	1970
Crew	31
Dimensions	265ft 9in x 31ft 2in x 26ft 3in (81m x 9.5m x 8m)
Displacement	
Surfaced	2,899 tons (2,845 tonnes)
Submerged	3,680 tons (3,739 tonnes)
Speed	14 knots
Surfaced	20 knots
Submerged	42 knots
Armament	6 x 21in (533mm) torpedo tubes; torpedoes; 36 mines
Powerplant	Liquid-metal reactor, two steam turbines
Range	Unlimited

testing at a depth of 3,280ft (1,000m), and the cheaper Akula class. Lack of funds precluded development of new boats for many years, but the improved circumstances of the former Soviet states may finally permit new classes of attack submarine to be considered. As these more advanced boats became available, older submarines were sold on to friendly governments. Significant numbers of Whiskey- and Romeo-class boats in particular were sold overseas. In some cases, these vessels were used to gain experience with submarines and a head start in the design stakes by nations with ambitions to create a powerful submarine force, but which did not want to start at the bottom of the learning curve.

The Soviet Union was successful to a great extent in concealing the capabilities of its boats. This forced NATO analysts to guess at what any given vessel was capable of. The distinctive pod mounted at the stern of the Sierra and Akula class attack submarines caused great consternation, for example. Theories about its function ranged from housing an advanced sensor array to some kind of new propulsion system.

Advanced Western Attack Submarines

The evolution of the attack

submarine continued throughout the Cold War period and afterward, though sometimes in fits and starts. World events and advancing foreign capabilities prompted new initiatives.

The Los Angeles-class attack submarine came about largely as a result of the realization that a U.S. carrier group could not outrun a Soviet November-class attack boat. The capabilities of the modern attack submarine were demonstrated in 1982 when a British nuclear sub, HMS *Conqueror*, torpedoed and sank the Argentinian cruiser *General Belgrano* during the Falklands War. The Argentine navy was large and powerful,

but was so intimidated by the threat of one or more nuclear boats outside its ports (in fact, *Conqueror* was alone at that point) that it did not come out to fight.

Large and Small

The last Cold War era attack submarine to come into service was the Seawolf class, which was designed in 1982. Large, fast, quiet, and enormously capable, Seawolf was designed to counter the best the Warsaw Pact could field, but entered service too late to play a part in the Cold War. The smallest class of nuclear attack submarine is the Rubis class built for the French navy. These boats date from the late 1970s, but have all been updated to the standards of the last-built boats, incorporating new technologies to create the Rubis/Amethyste class. Displacement is 2627 tons (2,670 tonnes) submerged,

about equivalent to a Thames-class fleet submarine of the 1930s and much larger than the typical wartime U-boat. The British Astute-class attack submarine is enormous by the standards of World War II boats, displacing some 7,400 tons (6,713 tonnes) submerged. It is hard to describe a vessel of this size, which is equivalent to a destroyer or cruiser, as a "boat," but the tradition endures.

Big boats are necessary to transport all the equipment and personnel required to carry out their role, or more accurately, roles. Today's Western attack submarines are likely to have to function in a variety of environments, including operating in shallow coastal waters. Since the 1991 Gulf War, attack submarines have conducted land attacks with missiles, and many boats can also launch missiles against enemy surface ships.

HMS *Astute*

Country	United Kingdom
Launch Date	2007
Crew	98
Dimensions	318ft x 37ft x 33ft
	(97m x 11.3m x 10m)
Displacement	
Surfaced	6,889 tons (7,000 tonnes)
Submerged	7,137 tons (7,400 tonnes)
Speed	
Submerged	29 knots
Armament	6 x 21in (533mm)
	torpedo tubes, 38
	Spearfish torpedoes,
	UGM-84 Harpoon and
	Tomahawk Block IV
	cruise missiles,
	naval mines
Powerplant	Rolls-Royce PWR2
	reactor, MTU diesel
	generators
Range	Circumnavigation 40
	times without
	refueling

ABOVE: The Los Angeles-class nuclear-powered attack submarine can launch cruise missiles from its torpedo tubes.

BELOW: The keel of HMS *Astute*, a nuclear-powered attack submarine, was laid down exactly a century from the date work began on the first Royal Navy submarine.

Chinese Military Submarines

Most of China's early subs came from the Soviet Union, including Romeo-class attack boats and plans for a Golf-class missile submarine. But cooling relations between China and the Soviet Union forced the Chinese to go it alone. China built a developed version of the Romeo class, which was capable of laying mines or undertaking a rather basic attack submarine role. The first Chinese nuclear attack boat was the Han class, built with German assistance. The Chinese settled for lower capabilities than other navies, perhaps seeing the Han class as a learning experience. Despite their relative simplicity, these boats are thought unreliable and accident-prone.

Gaining Experience

The Xia-class missile submarine was developed from the Han class and it, too, has had problems along the way. This is not uncommon with first-generation weapon systems, which the Xia is, to a great extent. Even though China entered the submarine warfare stakes late and benefited somewhat from the experiences of others, there is unquestionably no substitute for first-hand experience.

Second-generation boats are now entering service. The Shang-class attack boats are perhaps a generation behind U.S. attack submarines in terms of quietness and capability, but the Chinese navy is gaining experience that will permit the eventual development of world-class vessels.

Kilo Class

China also obtained a number of Kilo-class diesel-electric boats from Russia. The Kilo has been a considerable export success and may eventually form the basis of other classes developed overseas by purchasers. The Kilo class has a teardrop-shape hull form, which has more in common with Western boats than Russian designs. It is entirely likely that this will influence future Chinese submarine development.

Aspirational Fleet

Submarines are an important part of any modern navy, and China's interests in the Pacific seem to require an expanded fleet, so more submarines are likely to appear. It is not possible to enforce overseas territorial claims without a credible fleet, for example, and China's claim to the Spratly Islands is more likely to be upheld if backed by a modern blue-water navy. In any case, a powerful navy is seen as a status symbol and a deterrent against aggression by most powers, making continued naval expansion desirable if China's capabilities are to keep pace with her aspirations.

BELOW: The Chinese Navy's first nuclear-powered submarines were the Han class, introduced in the 1970s.

Kilo Class

Country	China
Launch Date	1980
Crew	45–50
Dimensions	226ft 5in x 29ft 6in x 23ft (69m x 9m x 7m)
Displacement	
Surfaced	2,454 tons (2,494 tonnes)
Submerged	3,053 tons (3,103 tonnes)
Speed	
Submerged	24 knots
Armament	Six x 21in (533mm) torpedo tubes
Powerplant	Single shaft, three diesels, three electric motors
Range	6,000nm (11,112km)

ABOVE: Kilo-class submarines can be easily identified by their tear-shaped hull.

LEFT: Of China's two Xia-class ballistic missile submarines, one is reported as having been lost because of an unspecified accident.

Special Operations Boats

Submarines are able to operate in areas a surface craft would be unable to enter, allowing them to carry out special operations or to gather intelligence about foreign vessels, seabed conditions, shore installations, and so forth.

Some of these missions can be carried out by any boat, though as a rule small diesel-electric submaines are better suited to covert coastal operations than large ocean-going nuclear attack boats. Some missions require a converted or custom-built vessel.

Special Operations

A submarine can act as a mobile listening post by riding at periscope depth with its antennae deployed and collecting enemy emissions. Much can be learned from the types of radar emitting in a given area even if communications cannot be intercepted and decoded. Some boats are able to deliver special forces teams. One conversion that has been used for this purpose was shelters on the deck of the submarine, in which special forces divers could ride as they approached the target, swimming out to fulfill their mission. Some special operations submarines have airlocks to permit divers to enter and exit the craft, carrying out sabotage or reconnaissance missions in hostile waters while the submarine waits nearby.

Small Saboteurs

Bottom-crawling submarines have also been considered for covert infiltration missions, either delivering teams to the land or conducting a covert mission in an enemy anchorage. None

of these roles really needs a full-scale submarine. Small special operations boats are easier to handle in coastal conditions and shallow water and are also cheaper to operate, freeing the attack submarines for more mainstream roles in fighting wars.

These small boats can be carried to their operational areas aboard larger vessels. For example, the Russian-India class submarine can carry special operations boats in place of her Deep Submergence Rescue Vehicles, delivering them to the target area and enabling them to make a speedy withdrawal after the mission.

The Sea Dagger submarine is a modular design that can be tailored to a range of activities by inserting the correct mission-specific module. It can function as a short-range attack boat or a swimmer delivery vehicle, reconnaissance platform, or training unit to assist in the development of antisubmarine techniques. At present, Sea Dagger is the only vessel of its type, but it is possible that more mission-configurable craft will become available in future.

ABOVE: The India class was designed for salvage and rescue operations but can also deliver special operations troops.

LEFT: U.S. Navy SEAL teams are trained to conduct demolitions and other special tasks underwater.

India Class

Country	Russia
Launch Date	1979
Crew	70
Dimensions	347ft 9in x 32ft 8in (106m x 10m)
Displacement	
Surfaced	3,200 tons (3,251 tonnes)
Submerged	4,000 tons (4,064 tonnes)
Speed	
Submerged	10 knots
Surfaced	15 knots
Armament	4 x 21in (533mm) torpedo tubes
Powerplant	Twin screws, diesel/ electric motors
Range	Not known

Modern Multirole Submarines

The majority of navies cannot afford to develop their own first-line attack submarines. In fact, few can afford to operate them even if they are purchased overseas. However, a submarine capability is an effective deterrent and is often seen as desirable.

Surplus Vessels

One solution is to buy surplus vessels from navies that are upgrading to newer designs, but such boats are usually well past their best. A range of vessels are available for export, which provide attack-sub capability at a fairly modest price. Boats of this type are mainly used for coastal patrols and defense of offshore assets, but can fulfill most war-fighting roles. Though lower in capability than a cutting-edge nuclear attack boat, they are equipped with modern sensors and fire-control electronics, creating a vessel that is vastly more capable than a second or third-hand surplus boat.

BELOW: Despite some technical problems, the Collins class is a highly effective diesel-electric attack boat built for the Royal Australian Navy.

German-designed submarines are in service with various nations, sometimes in modernized or modified form. The boats are offered in a range of configurations, allowing them to be tailored to the needs of the end user.

Types 206 and 209

The Type 206, which achieved considerable export success, was developed from a Cold War-era diesel attack boat intended for operations in the restricted waters of the Baltic. It was small and maneuverable, and these characteristics were inherited by its successor. Type 206s are gradually disappearing as they are replaced by more modern boats. In German service their replacement is the Type 212A. An export version with sensitive technologies replaced with more conventional systems, is now offered for export.

The larger Type 209 submarine has also been a big export success. Some versions can launch the submarine version of the Harpoon antiship missile; others mount only torpedoes. The Type 209 can be configured in various ways indicated by a second number after a slash, such as Type 209/1400. This indicates the submerged displacement of the vessel and gives general information of what systems are fitted.

RIGHT: The Type 206 is a successful modern diesel-electric design used by Germany and Israel. They can carry up to 24 mines externally.

BELOW: Designed in Germany with the export market in mind, the Type 209 design was based on the Type 206.

Schnorkel apparatus allows prolonged underwater operations.

Upgrades are available, allowing the Type 209 to use the most advanced torpedoes and, in some cases, missiles.

Conversion to Air Independent Propulsion (AIP) requires the insertion of a new section of hull.

Type 206

Country	Germany
Launch Date	1973
Crew	23
Dimensions	159ft 4in x 15ft 1in x 14ft 8in (48.6m x 4.6m x 4.5m)
Displacement	
Surfaced	450 tons (457 tonnes)
Submerged	500 tons (508 tonnes)
Speed	
Submerged	17 knots
Surfaced	10 knots
Armament	8 × 21in (533mm) t-tubes, 8 DM2A1 Seeaal (206)or DM2A3 Seehecht torpedoes; 24 mines
Powerplant	2 MTU 12V 493, four-stroke diesel engines, one Siemens-Schuckert-Werke electric motor
Range	Not known

Submarine and Antisubmarine Weapons

Some submarines can lay mines, and many can launch missiles. Ballistic missiles are strategic weapons and are of no real use in naval combat, but smaller missiles can be used to make "standoff" attacks against surface ships and even land targets.

Most submarine-launched missiles are developed from conventional naval missiles, such as Sub-Harpoon, which is the submarine version of the successful Harpoon missile. It is also possible to launch long-range cruise missiles, such as Tomahawk, from a submarine's torpedo tubes. Antiaircraft missile systems are not normally carried by submarines. Antiaircraft armament was useful for boats that spent most of their time on the surface but today's submarines do not. However, there are submarine-launched antiaircraft missile systems available. If fitted, they give a boat caught on the surface a chance to down a pursuing aircraft or helicopter and slip away before others arrive.

Torpedo Weights

Even though missiles offer a range of impressive capabilities, the weapon of choice is still the torpedo. There are two basic types—heavy and light.

BELOW: Sub-Harpoon missiles can be launched through the torpedo tube, ejecting their protective capsule before reaching the air.

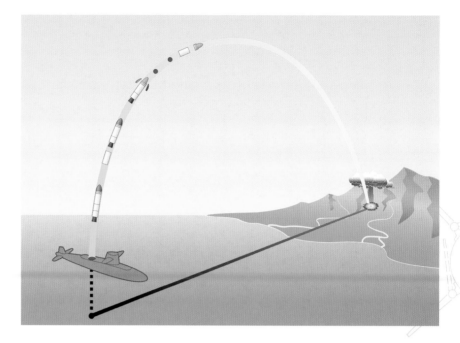

Lightweight torpedoes are often used as antisubmarine weapons, though they can attack vessels of all kinds. They are intended to attack by contact detonation, punching a hole in the enemy vessel's hull. Heavyweight torpedoes are intended to detonate under a surface ship. This creates a huge bubble of gas, which lifts the middle of the vessel. The weight of the ends may then break the vessel's back. Even if this does not occur, the shock of a nearby underwater explosion can severely damage a ship.

Most modern torpedoes are either guided or capable of autonomously homing in on the target. Some have reattack capability; that is, they can detect that they have missed and turn back for another pass. Torpedoes are also used to attack submarines. They may be dropped by aircraft, launched by CAPTOR

ABOVE: Submarine-launched ballistic missiles can attack land targets from a vast distance.

RIGHT: ASROC are "standoff" antisubmarine weapons, delivering a homing torpedo to the target vicinity by rapid airborne flight.

(CAPtive TORpedo) mines, or fired from a vessel or another submarine. ASROC (AntiSubmarine ROCket) weapons deliver a torpedo into the water some distance from the launching vessel. It then homes in on the target.

Less sophisticated antisubmarine weapons are still in use. These include pattern-dropped explosives launched from an antisubmarine rocket launcher and depth charges. Nuclear torpedoes and depth charges are available but would not normally be used except amid an all-out major war.

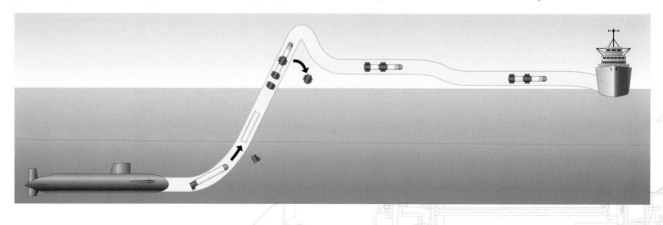

Propulsion, Sonar, and Stealth

The submarine's worst

enemy is noise. Any sound it makes can be used to detect, locate, and attack it. Similarly, all submarines carry sensitive instruments to listen for the noise of other vessels.

Ideally, a target can be detected and located with only passive measures (without making any sonar emissions that will give the sub's position away). If this is the case, the first indication that a sub is in the area may be the so-called "flaming datum"—a burning and sinking ship. All submarines are designed to be as quiet as possible, with machinery mounted on rubber blocks to reduce vibration wherever possible. Hulls are often coated with anechoic (sound-absorbing) materials that both deaden the boat's own sounds and reduce the returns from enemy active sonar.

Streamlined Silence

Another cause of noise is water turbulence caused by irregularities on the hull.

Vessels with a lot of openings and cavities produce a great deal of noise, especially at speed. Streamlined shapes and specially developed "slippery" materials reduce this noise. Cavitation is a problem for a boat moving fast. Cavitation occurs when a boat's screw (or screws) cause air bubbles to be formed due to low pressure behind the blade. The deeper a boat is, the greater the water pressure and thus the faster its screw can rotate without cavitating. Submarines use a single, large, slowly-rotating screw in preference to multiple smaller screws for this reason, and also to reduce turbulence in the boat's wake. Overall, a boat that is moving slowly is much harder to detect than one that is traveling fast. A submarine moving at flank speed may make enough noise that it cannot detect other boats, and is effectively "blind and deaf."

Sonar

The uses of sonar are not restricted to navigation and combat. Many submarines now mount mine-avoidance sonar, which gives warning of nearby objects. This is unlikely to be of use if the boat is traveling at speed, but when moving more cautiously it can assist in sneaking through a minefield or other obstructions. Ice-detection sonar fulfills a similar purpose. Sonar systems can be mounted in various ways. The optimum position for gathering data for an attack is the bow of the boat, with passive systems along the flanks where they can pick up noise from all around the boat. Some submarines also use a towed sonar array, which is trailed behind the boat. Each system has its own best position on the hull, depending on the job it is intended to do.

Yuri Dolgoruky

Country	Russia
Launch Date	February 2008
Crew	130
Displacement	
Surfaced	14,488 tons
	(14,720 tonnes)
Submerged	23,621 tons
	(24,000 tonnes)
Speed	
Surfaced	25 knots
Submerged	29 knots
Armament	16 × Bulava
	SLBMs, 6 × S-N-15
	cruise missiles, 21in
	(533mm) torpedo tubes
Powerplant	1 × OK-650B nuclear
	reactor, one AEU steam
	turbine, one shaft
Range	Unlimited except by
	food stores

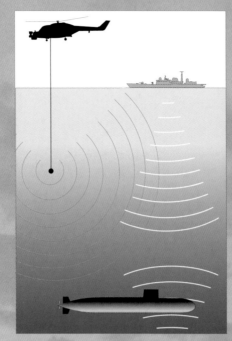

LEFT: Active sonar systems can be mounted on vessels or dipped into the sea from a hovering helicopter. Using active sonar gives away the emitter's position, so the decision to use it is a difficult one.

BELOW: Yuri Dolgoruky, lead ship of the Russian Borei-class ballistic missile submarine, is designed to have a minimal noise signature and active sonar return despite its size.

Civilian Submarines

Research and Commercial Usage

The possibility of an underwater transport vessel remains attractive for various reasons. Submarines are not greatly affected by storms on the surface and can move under pack ice, making them useful on the northern sea route around Siberia and in similar icebound regions.

Safety Requirements

As yet, this is not a reality, but civilian submarines are involved in tourism as well as civilian research and commercial activities. One major concern in such areas is safety; navies will accept risks that civilian operators (and their insurers) will not. In the event that a submarine sinks in deep water, there is little hope because the boat will pass crush depth and be destroyed. However, if it hits the bottom before this, the crew may be rescued. The ideal method is to use a rescue vehicle that docks with the submarine's escape hatch and takes off the crew in safety.

Escape Systems

The Russian India-class submarines were designed to transport such rescue craft to the scene of an accident and then act as a receiving station for survivors. Other Deep Submergence Rescue Vehicles are air-transportable and can be on-station to conduct a rescue within hours. There are other ways to get out of crippled submarines. Obviously, if diving suits are available, suitably trained personnel can use these to escape, but the majority of submariners cannot do so. From the early years of the twentieth century, various escape apparatus has been in use.

Davis Escape Apparatus

Personal submarine escape systems began in 1910, with the Davis escape apparatus, which combined a rebreather unit to clean the air with a life jacket. Various similar systems have been used worldwide, and have been proven to work down to a depth of about 656ft (200m). Modern equipment like the U.S. Submarine Escape Immersion Equipment (SEIE) includes thermal protection to prevent hypothermia in cold water and an inflatable life raft that can be used once the surface is reached.

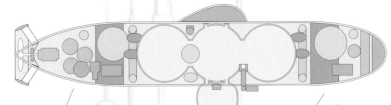

The vessel is operated by two crew, with two rescue personnel carried aboard and room for up to 24 other personnel.

The DRSV is designed to match the attitude of a submarine lying at an angle on the seabed.

ABOVE: The U.S. Navy's Mystic-class Deep Submergence Rescue Vehicle (DSRV) is carried to the rescue vicinity on a "mother sub," then detaches to approach the distressed vessel.

LEFT: The Davis escape apparatus, allowed sunken submariners a chance of escape, but only in fairly shallow water.

BELOW: Submarine Escape Immersion Equipment (SEIE) suits allow escape from sunken vessels and act as a life raft on the surface.

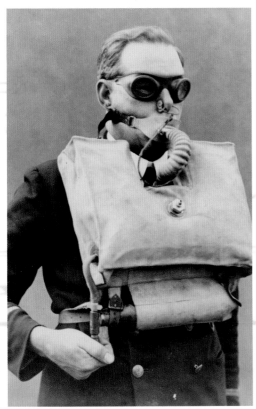

Wreck Location and Salvage

Salvage operations have been undertaken for as long as ships have existed, but up until the invention of the submarine, what could be achieved was strictly limited. Grabs lowered from surface vessels and divers swimming down to attach floats were the only real option.

Famous Wrecks

Since the submarine became available, it has become possible to locate and explore wrecks in very deep water, and sometimes to salvage them or at least bring up some artifacts. Perhaps the most famous wrecks in the world—the liner *Titanic* and the battleship *Bismarck*—were both located by Robert Ballard and explored by manned and remote-controlled submarines. Many other vessels have been located and explored, in some cases solving long-standing mysteries about their fate or the reasons for their sinking.

Remote Reconnaissance

Operating in a deep-water wreck is a hazardous business. The wreck itself is rarely in a safe condition and usually has numerous protrusions or narrow openings. The danger is compounded by poor visibility. Salvage submarines carry powerful lights because there is no natural light in deep water, but the water is not always clear. The submarine itself may disturb debris, and there are always seabed currents to deal with. These can not only churn up the seabed, but may cause a submersible to drift into tangled wreckage. For this reason, remote-controlled probes equipped with cameras and lights are used to explore many wrecks.

The best-known submarine-related salvage operation was carried out by a surface vessel, the *Glomar Explorer*. This vessel was custom-designed to retrieve the wreck of a Soviet Golf-class missile submarine from the ocean bed. The operation was a partial success. A cover story to maintain the secrecy of the operation suggested that *Glomar Explorer* was involved in seabed mining, attempting to retrieve manganese nodules from the seabed. This prompted interest in seabed mining. Exploration and prospecting operations are going on today, largely as a result of this invented story.

BELOW: The Phantom ROV (Remotely Operated Vehicle) enables wrecks to be investigated from the safety of a surface vessel.

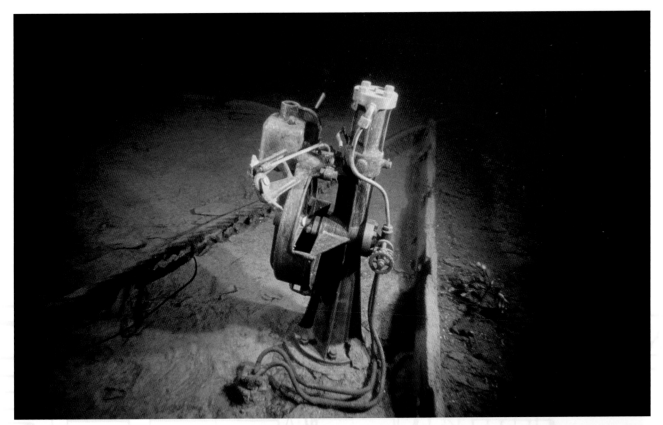

The deep-submergence vessel *Aluminaut*, built for exploration in waters of up to 14,763ft (4,500m) deep, was also involved in a novel salvage operation. In 1966, she assisted in the retrieval of a U.S. Air Force nuclear bomb that had fallen from a B-52 bomber after a midair collision. Three years later *Aluminaut* recovered another deep-ocean submersible from the Atlantic seabed.

ABOVE: The search for the wreck of RMS *Titanic* caused great leaps forward in underwater exploration. The ship's wheel can be seen in this picture.

RIGHT: USS *Bluegill* was sunk and used as a salvage training site for 13 years. In 1984, she was raised and moved to deep water, ending 42 years of service to the U.S. Navy.

Underwater Construction and Engineering Submarines

As the exploitation of deep waters continues to grow, submarines are increasingly necessary to assist in the construction and maintenance of structures and equipment. There is a limit to how deep divers can go and how long they stay down; a submarine allows missions of longer duration at greater depth. Submarines are used for survey work before a project begins and to support divers where appropriate. A detailed map of the seabed, water pressure and temperature conditions, salinity, currents, and similar oceanographic data must be taken into consideration before a project can start. There is at present a fair amount of controversy over seabed mining and similar commercial operations, so it is likely that research will have to be undertaken into local ecological conditions before a project can proceed.

Survey and Safety

Once the project has actually begun, submarines permit a number of activities to be carried out with relative ease. Inspections of underwater pipelines and cables as well as the underwater components of oil-drilling rigs can be efficiently carried out by crewed or remotely controlled vessels, and repairs can be made as necessary. Inspections of damage can also be made in the event that an accident occurs, increasing safety and reducing costs. Increasing use is being made of deep-diving robots for this kind of work. Known as ROVs (Remotely Operated Vehicles), these are essentially robotic submarines and do much the same work as a manned craft. At present, remotely controlled robotic vessels are standard, but there are hopes that in the near future fully autonomous craft can be introduced to handle routine work and thus free up assets for more complex tasks elsewhere.

Depth Advancement

The difficulties inherent in underwater engineering are similar to those that beset salvage and wreck location missions. Working in deep, dark water in close proximity to the legs of a drilling rig or the seabed can be hazardous

and requires considerable skill just to keep the submarine safe. If complex work must also be undertaken—often requiring very precise positioning of the craft—then the difficulty increases still further.

It is thought that there are vast mineral resources and large oil fields to be exploited on the seabed. Much of this wealth lies in very deep water.

The world's need for resources is set to continue increasing, so it is only logical that deep-water projects will become ever more important to the world economy, and that in turn will require ever more advanced vehicles to allow people to work in the depths of the seas.

Submarines continue to be an invaluable investment in the twenty-first century and development of these colossal vessels is ongoing.

TOP LEFT: Semisubmersible oil platforms can transit relatively shallow waters, taking on seawater as ballast to increase their draft.

TOP: The oil industry makes use of a range of remotely operated vehicles for underwater work and inspection.

ABOVE: The Deep Rover submersible allows a single operator to undertake precision work in 3,280ft (1,000m) of water. It is designed to be no more difficult to operate than driving a car.

 Civilian Submarines

Index

Page numbers in *italics* refer to illustrations

A-class submarines (UK) *9*, 26, 30
Air-Independent Propulsion (AIP) systems 11–12, 66
aircraft, threat to submarines 39, 44
Akula-class submarines (Russia) 58, 59
Alfa-class submarines (Russia) 58, 59
Aluminaut 77
anti-submarine warfare (ASW) 58, 68, *69*
Aquarius underwater laboratory 74
Argentina 51, 60
Argonaut, USS 23
ASDIC 12, 29, 33
ASROC (anti-submarine rocket) 68, *69*
Astute class submarines (UK) 60, *61*
attack submarines 52, 58–9, 60, *61*
Australia *66*
Austro-Hungary 30

B-class submarines (UK) 26, 30
Baker, George 23
Ballard, Robert 76
Baltic Sea 30, 46, 66
Bismarck 76
Bluegill, USS 77
Bourne, William 16
Brandtaucher 18–19
Brin class submarines (Italy) 41

CAPTOR (Captive Torpedo) mines 68
China 62, *63*
civilian submarines 72–9
Cold War *6–7*, 51, 52–63, 66, *67, 70–1*
Collins-class submarines (Australia) *66*
components of a submarine 8–9
Conqueror, HMS 60
crush depth 8–9

D-class submarines (UK) 27, 30, *31*
David, CSS 20, *21*
Davis escape apparatus 72, 73
deck guns 13, *29, 37*, 41
deep-ocean exploration 74, 75, *76–7*
Deep Rover submersible *79*
Deep Submergence Rescue Vehicles (DSRV)
  72, 73
depth charges 29, 32, 39, 68
depth control 9–10, *11*
Deutschland 28, 34
Diable Marin 19
diesel engines 10–11, 27, 28, 52, 58
double hulls 9, 28, 38, 45
Drebbel, Cornelius 16

E-class submarines (UK) 28, 30, *31, 37*
earliest submarines 8–9, 16–17
Enrico Toti class submarines (Italy) 52, *53*
escape systems 72, *73*
Excalibur, HMS 50, *51*
Explorer, HMS 50, *51*

Falklands War (1982) 51, 60
Fenian Ram 24
Fisher, Admiral Sir John 'Jacky' 24
Florida, USS *6–7*, 12
France
  Cold War 60
  Gustave Zede 22–3
  Gymnote 22, *23*
  Le Plongeur 19
  Nautilus 18
  Surcouf 38, *39*
  World War I 26, 30, *31*
  World War II 38, *39*, 40, 42
Frimaire class submarines (French) 30
Fulton, Robert 18, 19

Gato-class submarines (US) 42, *43*
General Belgrano 60
Germany
  Brandtaucher 18–19
  Cold War 66, *67*
  World War I 28–9, 32–3, 34
  World War II 40, *41*, 44–5, 56
Glomar Explorer 76
Golf-class submarines (Russia) 62, 76
Gotland class submarines (Sweden) *11*
Goubert, Claude 22
Grayback, USS 56, 57
Gulf War (1991) 60

Gustave Zede 22–3
Gymnote 22, *23*

Hairredin Barbarossa 30
Halibut, USS 57
Han-class submarines (China) 62
hand-powered submarines 8, 10, 17
Holland, John Philip 24, *25*
Holland 1 24
Holland VI 24, *26*
Housatonic, USS 21
Hunley, CSS *14–15*, 20–1
Hunley, Horace 20, 21
hydrogen peroxide propulsion 11, 44–5, 50
hydrography 44
hydroplanes 16, 17

I-400 class submarines (Japan) 49
India-class submarines (Russia) 65, 72
Intelligent Whale 18, 19
Italy 30, 40–1, 52, 53

J-class submarines (UK) 36
Japan 41, 42, 46, 48–9
JIM diving suit 75

K-class submarines (UK) 34–5
Kaiten human torpedoes 48, *49*
Kilo-class submarines (Russia) 58, 62, *63*

L-class submarines (US) 36
L10 (UK) 36
Le Plongeur 19
Los Angeles class attack submarines (US) 60, *61*

M-1, USS *38–9*
M-class submarines (UK) 35, 38
M1 (UK) *35*
M2 (UK) *34*
'milk cows' 40
mine-laying submarines 13, 38, 46, 62
mineral prospecting 76, 78–9
missile-launching submarines *6–7*, 13 56–7, 62, 63,
  66, 68, *70–1*
MK37 torpedo *13*
Mystic class Deep Submergence Rescue Vehicle (US) *72, 73*

NATO 51, 54, 56
Nautilus, USS (1954) 54
Nautilus (1800) 18, *19*
noise reduction 12, 70, *71*
Nordenfelt submarines 22
November-class submarines (Russia) 54, *55*, 60
nuclear missiles 56–7
nuclear power
  attack submarines 58–9, 60, *61*
  introduction of 10, 11, 52, 54

Ohio class ballistic missile submarine (US) *6–7*, 12
oil-drilling rigs 78
Oldenburg 34

periscope *12*
Phantom Remotely Operated Vehicle 76
Pioneer (1862) 20
Plunger, USS 24
Pluviose class submarines (French) *31*

Q-ships 32

R-class submarines (UK) 36
radar *39*
Regulus missiles 56, *57*
remote-controlled submarines 74, 76, 78, 79
Remotely Operated Vehicles (ROVs) *76*, 78, *79*
Resurgam 8, 22
Romeo-class submarines (Russia) 59, 62
Rotterdam Boat 16
Royal Oak, HMS 40
Rubis class submarines (France) 60
Russia
  Cold War 51, 52, 54, *55*, 58–9, 60, 62, *70–1*
  World War I 30
  World War II 46

S-class submarines (UK) 42, *43*, 46
Scapa Flow 40
schnorkel equipment 11, 44, 45
Sea Dagger-class submarines (Sweden) 65
Seal, USS *26–7*, 36

seaplane-carrying submarines 34, 48–9
Seawolf class submarines (US) 60
Shang-class submarines (China) 62
Sierra-class submarines (Russia) 58–9
Skate, USS 52–3
Sonar 12–13, 29, 33, 54, 70, *71*
special operations 48, 57, 64–5
steam powered boats *8*, 10, 22–3, *24, 31*, 35, 52
Stingray torpedo *13*
Sub-Harpoon anti-ship missile 66, 68
Submarine Escape Immersion Equipment (SEIE) *72, 73*
Surcouf 38, *39*
Sweden *11*, 22, 51, 65

tactics
  Cold War 51, 54
  unrestricted submarine warfare 29, 32
  wolf-packs 44
  World War I 27, 28, 29, 30, 33, 38
  World War II 40, 41, 42, 44, 46
Thames class submarines (UK) 42, 60
Thermocline *12*
Titanic, RMS 76, *77*
Tomahawk missile 57, 68
torpedoes
  Cold War 54, 58
  human torpedoes 48, *49*
  modern 13, 68
  nuclear 54, 68
  spar torpedo 20, 21
  Whitehead Automotive Torpedo 22
  World War I 28, 30, *31*, 38
  World War II 42, 44, 48
Trident missile *13*
Tuck, Josiah 22
Turkey 30
Turtle 17
Type VIIC U-boat 40, *41*, 42
Type XVIII U-boat 45
Type XXI U-boat 45
Type 206 submarines (Germany) 66, *67*
Type 209 submarines (Germany) 66
Type 212A submarines (Germany) 66

U-1 28
U-9 28
U-21 28
U-35 28
U-47 40, *41*
U-139 32–3
U-155 28
U-class submarines (UK) 46, *47*
UB-14 28
Unbeaten, HMS *39*
underwater construction and engineering submarines 78–9
United, HMS *46–7*
United Kingdom
  Drebbel submarines 16
  Falklands War (1982) 51, 60
  World War I *9*, 26, 27, 28, 30, *31*, 34–6, 37, 38
  World War II 40, 42, 43, 46, *47*, 48
United States
  Argonaut, USS 23
  Civil War *14–15*, 20–1
  Cold War *6–7*, 52–3, 56, *57*, 60, *61*
  Holland submarines 24
  Intelligent Whale 18, 19
  Turtle 17
  World War I *26–7*, 32, 36, *38–9*
  World War II 42, 43, 44, 46
unrestricted submarine warfare 29, 32
US Navy SEALs 64–5

Ventose 31
Verne, Jules 18, 22, 23

Warsaw Pact 51, 54, 56–7, 58
Whiskey-class submarines (Russia) 59
Whitehead Automotive Torpedo 22
World War I *9*, 26–37, 38
World War II 38–49, 56
wreck location and salvage 76–7

X-craft (UK) 48
Xia-class submarines (China) 62, *63*

Yuri Dolgoruky 70–1

Zalinski Boat 24
Zede, Gustave 22

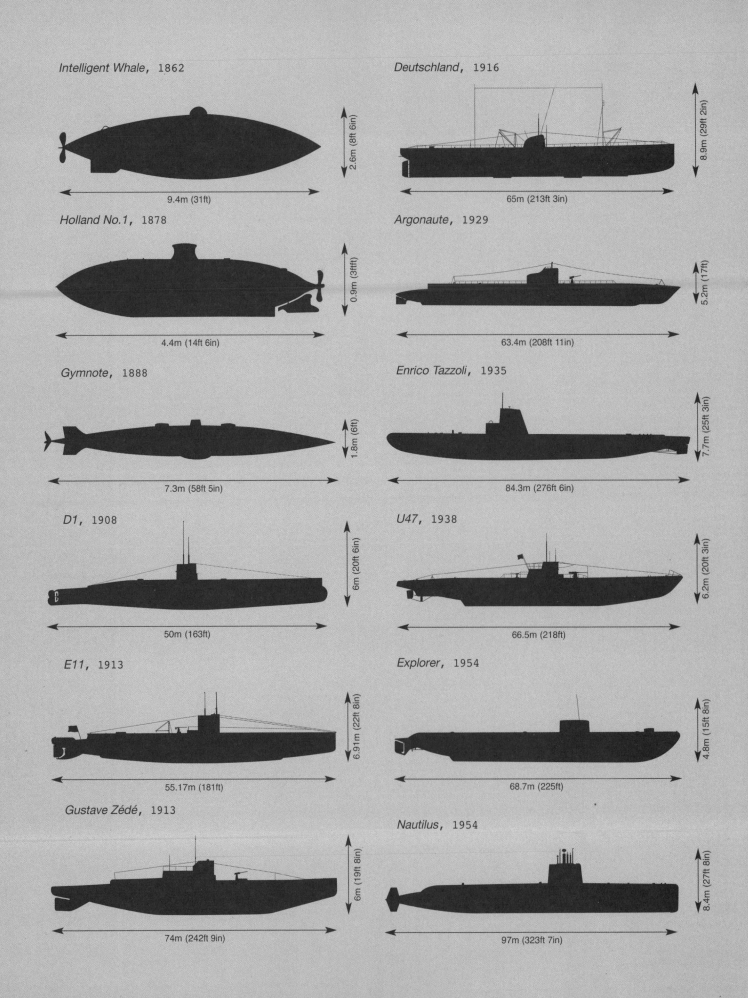

Intelligent Whale, 1862
2.6m (8ft 6in)
9.4m (31ft)

Deutschland, 1916
8.9m (29ft 2in)
65m (213ft 3in)

Holland No.1, 1878
0.9m (3ftft)
4.4m (14ft 6in)

Argonaute, 1929
5.2m (17ft)
63.4m (208ft 11in)

Gymnote, 1888
1.8m (6ft)
7.3m (58ft 5in)

Enrico Tazzoli, 1935
7.7m (25ft 3in)
84.3m (276ft 6in)

D1, 1908
6m (20ft 6in)
50m (163ft)

U47, 1938
6.2m (20ft 3in)
66.5m (218ft)

E11, 1913
6.91m (22ft 8in)
55.17m (181ft)

Explorer, 1954
4.8m (15ft 8in)
68.7m (225ft)

Gustave Zédé, 1913
6m (19ft 8in)
74m (242ft 9in)

Nautilus, 1954
8.4m (27ft 8in)
97m (323ft 7in)